P9-CQB-446

3 MINUTE
AESOP'S FABLES

Retold by Gina Phillips

Illustrated by F.S. Persico

kidsbooks®
Incorporated

Copyright © 1991 by Kidsbooks Inc.
7004 N. California Ave.
Chicago, IL 60645

All rights reserved including the right
of reproduction in this or in any other form.

Manufactured in the United States of America

The Lion and the Mouse

One afternoon, a large, shaggy lion was sleeping in the shade when a tiny mouse ran across his nose. The lion woke up with a great start and roared, "Who dares awaken the king of the jungle?" The lion looked down just in time to clamp his huge paw over the mouse.

"Oh, please forgive me!" cried the terrified mouse as he struggled to get loose. "I promise never to waken you again."

"You certainly won't," said the lion, "because I'm going to eat you right now."

The poor mouse pleaded for his life and promised to help the lion someday if only the lion would spare his life. Amused by the thought of needing help from such a tiny creature, the lion decided to let the little mouse go free. "Besides," the lion said with a laugh, "you would not even make a decent mouthful."

One night a few weeks later the mouse was hunting for food when he heard the lion roaring. The roars became louder and stronger as the mouse hurried toward the sound. In a clearing, he found the lion caught in a hunter's rope net. The more the lion struggled, the more tangled up he became.

"Don't worry," said the mouse. "I shall help you."

"What can you possibly do to help me," roared the lion, "when all my strength has not been enough to rip this net."

"Just be patient," replied the mouse. "I promised to repay you for sparing my life and so I shall." Then the mouse quickly began to chew through the ropes one by one until the lion was free. "There! You're free," said the mouse, tired but proud.

The lion gently picked up the mouse in his paw. "You have more than repaid a favor," said the grateful lion. "You have saved my life."

Do not judge a person's usefulness by his appearance.

The Fox and the Grapes

One hot summer afternoon there was a very hungry fox who had been searching the woods all day for a rabbit or a fat squirrel.

"At least I shall have a nice cool drink," said the fox as he headed for his favorite water hole. But when he arrived, he found that the water hole had dried up and there was not a drop to drink.

Now the fox was thirsty as well as hungry. Deeper and deeper into the forest he wandered. After a while he came to a large vine-covered tree, and hearing a noise, he looked up to see a crow perched on a low branch eating some grapes.

The hungry fox eyed the crow carefully. "Even a skinny old crow like you looks like a tempting meal today," he said.

"Oh, no, you don't," cried the crow as he flew to a higher branch well out of reach of the fox's sharp teeth.

At that moment the fox noticed the beautiful grapes the crow had been eating. "Ah!" said the fox. "At last I shall have something to eat. These grapes look so juicy they will satisfy my thirst as well."

The crow looked down at the fox far below and croaked, "You won't dine on these grapes either—they are too high for you to reach!"

"Oh, really," growled the fox. "Just watch me!"

The fox stretched himself as tall as he could on his hind legs, but even though he stood on the tips of his toes, he could not reach the grapes. Next he ran at the tree and jumped as high as he could, but he still was not able to reach the ripe, juicy grapes that hung above his head. Again and again he jumped, but to no avail. The exhausted fox finally lay panting on the ground.

From high up in the tree the crow laughed and laughed.

"Oh, I didn't really want those grapes," said the fox. "Anyone can see they are as sour as lemons."

Some people pretend to despise the things they cannot have.

The City Mouse and the Country Mouse

Once upon a time there was a country mouse who lived a simple but happy life in the fields and woods. Under a hedge he had a little straw nest that was soft and warm.

One day the country mouse decided to invite his cousin, who lived in the city, for a visit. When the city mouse arrived, the country mouse did everything possible to make his cousin's stay enjoyable. The country mouse brought out all the food he had worked so hard to gather—nuts, berries, grain, and even a small apple he had dragged home from the orchard.

The elegant city mouse only picked at the food. In fact, he ate hardly anything. The city mouse finally said, "Cousin, how can you bear to eat such plain, dull food? And if that is not bad enough, there is nothing around here but meadows and trees. It's so boring. You should see where I live! There are people and carriages and lights and food—such wonderful food—just there for the taking. You don't even have to work for it."

The city mouse painted such a beautiful picture with his words that the country mouse agreed to move to the city with him at once. When the cousins arrived in the city, they went to the huge house where the city mouse lived. The country mouse looked around in wonder, for everything was just as the city mouse had described. There were velvet drapes, soft rugs, and best of all, a dining room with a table covered with leftover food.

The two mice jumped on the table and began to eat cheese and turkey, grapes and bread. The country mouse could hardly believe his good fortune when suddenly the door opened and a group of laughing people walked in to finish their feast. The terrified mice leaped off the table and hid behind a cabinet. After a long time, the people finally left. Just as the mice came crawling out a huge cat leaped across the room and almost caught them in its sharp claws.

"That's enough for me!" cried the frightened country mouse. "I'm going back to my peaceful country home, where the food may be plain but I can eat it without fear!"

For some a safe, simple life is better than a rich life full of danger.

The Eagle and the Crow

A crow was sitting on a tree branch, when he spied an eagle landing on the ground below him. The eagle was carrying a large nut in his beak. The eagle tried to break open the nut by banging it on the ground. The crow watched as the eagle tried and tried to crack the shell, and he wondered how he might take the nut away from the powerful eagle. Finally the crow said, "I don't think you'll ever open the nut like that."

"Oh, really," said the eagle in an annoyed tone of voice, and with that he tried again even harder. He did everything he could think of and still the nut would not open. After a while the eagle looked up at the crow, and although he hated to ask, he said, "What would you do in my place?"

"Well," said the wily crow, "if I were you, I'd fly high in the sky with the nut and then drop it onto the rocks over there." With one wing the crow pointed to a large group of boulders nearby. "It's the only way that hard shell will ever crack," said the crow.

"I must admit you have a good idea," said the eagle. And with that, the eagle grabbed the nut in his strong claws and flew high in the sky. The crow watched the eagle become smaller and smaller as he flew higher and higher. Then at last, when the eagle was just a speck in the sky, he let go of the nut. Down it dropped, down, down onto the rocks. Sure enough, when the nut hit the rocks it cracked open just as the crow had said it would.

Because the eagle was so high in the sky, he took a long time to return. Meanwhile, the crow hopped over to the broken nut, gobbled up the sweet kernel, and flew off chuckling to himself.

By the time the eagle flew back down, he found nothing left but pieces of broken shell.

Before accepting advice, it is wise to consider the source.

The Wolf and the Kid

Once upon a time there was a mother goat who lived with her kid in a little cottage at the edge of the forest. Each day the mother goat would leave her kid alone in the cottage while she went off to a meadow nearby to feed upon the sweet grass that grew there.

Before she left, she always made sure the door was shut tight and locked. She called back to her kid and said, "Make sure the door is bolted on the inside and whatever you do, don't let anyone in while I am gone—not anyone. The old wolf is always looking for a tasty meal. When I return I will knock three times so you will know it is me. Then you can safely open the door."

The kid promised to remember the mother goat's instructions and so she went off to the meadow knowing her baby was safe. Now, it so happened that the wolf had been hiding behind the hedge in the yard and overheard every word the mother goat had said to her kid.

"Ah-ha!" muttered the wolf. "I shall soon have a delicious lunch!" He waited a short while and then walked boldly up to the cottage door. Knock, knock, knock. The wolf hit the door three times. He made his voice sound like the mother goat's voice and said, "I'm home from the meadow. You can let me in now."

The wolf was very impatient, and when the door did not open at once, he said in his sweetest voice, "Hurry up, daughter dear, before the nasty old wolf gets me."

The kid came to the door and was just about to open it when she thought to herself, "My mother came home very quickly—usually she is gone much longer than this.

Perhaps I'd better check to see who's out there before I unlock the door." The kid stood on her hind legs and peered out the window. Sure enough, she saw the wolf by the front door. "Go away!" yelled the kid. "You may sound like a goat, but you look like a wolf. Go try your tricks on someone else."

Better to be safe
than sorry.

The Hare and the Tortoise

Once there was a hare who was very proud of how fast he could run. The hare boasted to all the other animals about his speed, but he especially liked to brag in front of the tortoise, who could only walk—and quite slowly at that.

One day the tortoise said, "It is true that I am slow, but I could beat you in a race."

"Never!" said the hare, who was greatly amused at the very thought.

"Then let us race to the other side of the valley," said the tortoise.

"Agreed," said the hare.

The tortoise and the hare started off together, but with his great speed the hare was soon out of sight. The tortoise plodded slowly along behind. It was such a hot day and the hare was so far ahead that he decided to stop and take a little nap. The hare knew he could beat the tortoise even if he rested for a while. The hare lay down and quickly fell asleep. Meanwhile, the tortoise continued to walk slowly and steadily throughout the day.

The hare slept longer than he intended. When he awoke he realized that the tortoise had passed him. "Not to worry," thought the hare, "I shall catch up in no time." And off he went, leaping over brooks and bushes with speed and grace.

The hare ran as fast as he could and soon reached the other side of the valley. Up ahead he could see all the other animals cheering. The hare quickly reached the end of the race only to find that the tortoise crossed the finish line ahead of him.

Slow and steady can win the race.

The Boy Who Cried Wolf

Once there was a shepherd boy who looked after all the sheep that belonged to his village. Each morning he would collect the sheep and take them into the hills to feed, and each evening he would carefully round them up and bring them home again.

After doing this for many months the shepherd boy grew bored. One day he decided to cause a little excitement. "Wolf! Wolf!" he cried in his loudest voice.

At once all the men in the village raced out of their barns with pitchforks in their hands and ran to save the sheep. But when they reached the shepherd boy there was no wolf, and the boy rolled on the ground laughing at how he had fooled the entire village.

It was such a good trick and so much fun that the boy did it again a few days later. "Wolf! Wolf!" he yelled. As before, the villagers rushed to help him, only to discover that the boy had fooled them once again.

The following week, just as it was getting dark and the shepherd was gathering the sheep for the trip home, he heard a frightened "Baa!" from one of the sheep. As the boy looked toward the sound he saw a low, dark shape at the edge of the meadow. The boy realized it was a wolf and became very afraid, for he had only his staff for protection. As the wolf crept closer and closer the boy cried out, "Wolf! Wolf! Wolf!" in his loudest voice. But this time no one came. Everyone in the village thought the boy was playing another one of his jokes. Even though the shepherd boy screamed and screamed, no one came to help.

The boy escaped, ran back to the village, and convinced someone to help him, but by the time he returned, the wolf and all the sheep were gone.

A liar will not be believed even when he speaks the truth.

15

The Sun and the Wind

Once upon a time the wind bragged to the sun about his great strength. "See how I can bend the strongest trees and watch how I can strip the leaves from their branches," said the wind.

The sun replied that he could melt the snow and make the flowers grow.

"That is true," said the wind, "but I am much more powerful than you and I shall prove it. See that traveler wearing a cape down there? The one who can get his cape off is the strongest. Agreed?"

"That seems fair to me," said the sun. "You can try first."

The wind gathered all his forces and started to blow as hard as he could. Great black clouds rolled across the sky and it grew very dark. The wind blew so hard he bent the trees and even caused some of them to break. Leaves swirled all around, but the stronger the wind blew, the more the traveler clutched his cape. In fact, it became so cold that the traveler wrapped himself in his cape even tighter than usual. Finally the wind gave up and told the sun to take his turn.

The sun put a smile on his round face and beamed down on the traveler. The storm clouds disappeared and the air became soft and warm. This sudden change in the weather surprised the traveler and pleased him greatly.

As the traveler walked on, the sun continued to shine, and its rays warmed the traveler so much that before long he took off his cape and tucked it under his arm.

At that moment, the sun smiled gently at the wind, and there was never again another argument about who was the strongest.

Gentleness is often more effective than force.

The Goose and the Golden Eggs

One day a farmer went to the market to buy a goose for his barnyard. The goose looked like any other goose, except for one thing. When the farmer went out to the barn the next morning, he discovered that the goose had laid a golden egg.

The farmer could hardly believe his eyes. He called his wife to come see the incredible egg. The farmer's wife hurried over and she too was amazed to see the beautiful golden egg. "I wonder if the goose will lay another," she said to her husband.

Sure enough, the next morning there was another golden egg, then another and another. The farmer's wife moved the goose into the house and gave it a box of soft straw next to the fireplace. She fed the goose the best grain and the freshest water. In return the goose laid a golden egg each morning.

After a time the farmer's wife said, "Someday we shall be rich, but it will take too long, and by the time we save up enough eggs they will not be worth half of what they are today. I have an idea. Inside the goose must be a great number of golden eggs. Why should we have to wait for them? Bring me a knife and we'll have all the gold at once."

Now, the goose had been a good and dependable bird, and the farmer did not like his wife's idea. Nevertheless, he did as she asked. He killed the goose and cut her open. Inside, the goose was just like any other goose and there were no golden eggs to be found.

Don't be greedy.

Belling the Cat

A long time ago there was a great gathering of mice. The mice had come together to try to find a way to keep themselves safe from their enemy, the cat. They sat around the barn in a big circle wiggling their whiskers and swishing their long tails and looking very important indeed.

Some mice said "Let's do this," and others said "Let's do that," but no one idea appealed to all of them. Suddenly a young mouse called Bright Eyes drew himself up very tall and said in a loud voice, "I have the answer that will keep us safe from the cat for all time."

"What is it? What is it?" squeaked all the other mice.

"Well," said Bright Eyes, "the main reason we get caught so often by the cat is that the cat moves so quietly she is upon us before we have a chance to escape."

"True! True!" shouted all the other mice at once.

"If we found a way to know when the cat is coming," continued Bright Eyes, "we could scatter and hide and not ever get caught again. Here is my idea. I propose that we get a small bell and tie it around the cat's neck with a ribbon. The moment the cat makes the slightest movement, the bell will ring and we will be warned in plenty of time to escape. The cat will never be able to sneak up on us again."

"What a great idea!" the other mice exclaimed. Happy that a solution had finally been found, they began to talk excitedly about whether the bell should be brass or silver and what color ribbon they should use.

Sitting in a corner all this time was a very old mouse, who had listened carefully to everything that had been said. The old mouse finally spoke up. "What Bright Eyes has suggested is all very well, but please tell me who is going to put the bell on the cat."

The moment the old mouse's words were heard, all the other mice—especially Bright Eyes—felt very foolish and embarrassed, for not one of them was willing to volunteer to place the bell around the cat's neck.

It is easier to talk about doing great deeds than it is to accomplish them.

The Grasshopper and the Ant

There was once a fine green grasshopper who could sing and dance with great skill. One summer day the grasshopper happened upon an ant who was pushing a grain of corn up a hill. The grasshopper stopped to watch the ant as he struggled and sweated in the hot sun, hauling grain after grain up the hill.

Finally the grasshopper asked the ant what he was doing. The ant replied that he was gathering food for the winter and storing it in his nest at the top of the hill.

"Winter!" The merry grasshopper laughed. "Winter is so far away. Why don't you stop and enjoy the day with me?"

"No, no," said the ant. "I really must gather all the food I can, for I have many mouths to feed at home." And the ant continued to work.

The grasshopper laughed once again and danced away. The ant could hear him singing as he went. All through the summer the ant worked. The grasshopper tried many times to get the ant to play, but to no avail.

Soon the summer became fall, and the ant worked even harder. There were ripe berries now and wonderful seeds to bring back to his nest. Meanwhile the grasshopper continued to play, and his singing became even more beautiful.

Then one night the cold wind blew, and in the morning a heavy frost covered the land. The grasshopper finally realized he must gather food for the winter. Although he searched everywhere, he could not find a thing—not a seed or a berry or a grain. It was too late. The ant and the other animals had already taken all the food and stored it for the cold months ahead.

The weather became colder and colder and the grasshopper grew more and more hungry. Finally he could stand it no longer, and he went to the ant to beg for some food. The ant said, "I worked all summer for my food while you laughed at me. What did you do?"

"I danced and sang all summer," replied the grasshopper in a small voice.

"Well, then," said the ant, "you can continue to dance and sing all winter, too, for I shall not give you a thing." And with that, the ant went back into his warm, cozy nest.

Don't put off till tomorrow what you must do today.